WORKING PAPER
ALFRED P. SLOAN SCHOOL OF MANAGEMENT

Cooperation Between Competing Firms: Informal Know-How Trading

Eric von Hippel

March 1986   WP # 1759-86

MASSACHUSETTS
INSTITUTE OF TECHNOLOGY
50 MEMORIAL DRIVE
CAMBRIDGE, MASSACHUSETTS 02139

Cooperation Between Competing Firms:
Informal Know-How Trading

Eric von Hippel

March 1986   WP # 1759-86

This research is supported by a grant from the Division of Policy
Research and Analysis, The National Science Foundation.

ABSTRACT

"Informal" know-how trading is the extensive exchange of proprietary know-how by informal networks of process engineers in competing firms. We have observed such know-how trading networks to be very active in the US steel minimill industry and elsewhere, and they appear to represent a novel form of cooperative R&D.

When we examine technology trading in the framework of a "Prisoner's Dilemma", real-world conditions can be specified where informal trading of proprietary know-how with direct competitors both does and does not make economic sense from the point of view of participating firms. Data available to date on the presence and absence of such trading appears to be roughly in accordance with the predictions of this model.

Cooperation Between Competing Firms:
Informal Know-How Trading

1.0: Introduction

It has long been recognized that it is difficult for an innovating firm to fully appropriate the benefits arising from its innovations, and that desired research might therefore not be performed (1). One sometimes possible solution to this dilemma is cooperative R&D conducted by firms who share the costs and benefits of particular R&D projects (2).

In this paper we explore a novel type of cooperative R&D: the informal trading of proprietary know-how between directly competing firms. We have observed this behavior to be widespread in at least one industry. We propose that the phenomenon makes economic sense, and that it has interesting properties from the point of view of innovation research and practice.

We begin by briefly characterizing informal technology trading as we have observed it to date (section 2). Next, we present a case study of this behavior involving the trading of proprietary process know-how among competing US steel minimill firms (section 3). Then, we explore whether and when technology trading between direct competitors is an economically advantageous form of cooperative R&D from the viewpoint of individual participating firms (section 4). Finally, we consider the relationship of R&D trading to other forms of cooperative R&D and suggest patterns in such trading which we might expect to observe in real-world industries (section 5).

I would like to express my thanks to Professor Richard Nelson of Yale for his helpful comments. My thanks also to the MIT Sloan School of Management Graduate Students who helped in the research during the past two years via data collection and stimulating discussion: John Becker, Alan Drane, Abbie Griffin, Howard Levine, Gordon Low, Richard Orr, and Heidi Sykes-Gomez.

2.0: A General Description of Informal Know-How Trading

Know-how is the accumulated practical skill or expertise which allows one to do something smoothly and efficiently. The know-how which we focus on here is that held in the minds of a firm's engineers who develop its products and develop and operate its processes. Often, a firm considers a significant portion of such know-how proprietary and protects it as a trade secret.

A firm's staff of engineers is responsible for obtaining or developing the know-how its firm needs. When required know-how is not available in-house, an engineer typically cannot find it in publications either: Much is very specialized and not published anywhere. He must either develop it himself or learn what he needs to know by talking to other specialists. Since in-house development can be time-consuming and expensive, there can be a high incentive to seek the needed information from professional colleagues. And often, logically enough, engineers in competing firms which make similar products or use similar processes are the people most likely to have that needed information. But are these professional colleagues willing to reveal their proprietary know-how to employees of competing firms? Interestingly, it appears that the answer is quite uniformly "yes" in at least one industry, and quite probably in many.

The informal proprietary know-how trading behavior which we have observed to date can be characterized as an informal trading "network" which develops between engineers having common professional interests. In general, such trading networks appear to be formed and refined as engineers get to know each other at professional conferences. When a network is built on contacts derived from conferences which focus on a technology which is essentially unique to one industry (for example, the "Melter's Guild" of steel furnace operators), network members would largely consist of professionals employed by directly competing firms. When conferences important to formation of a particular network

are based on a technical interest which spans many industries (for example, the Materials Research Society), network membership will span competing and noncompeting firms.

Network formation begins when, at conferences and elsewhere, an engineer builds his personal informal list of possibly useful expert contacts by making private judgments as to the areas of expertise and abilities of those he meets. Later, when "Engineer A" encounters a product or process development problem he finds difficult, he activates his network by calling Engineer B, an appropriately knowledgeable contact who works at a competing (or noncompeting) firm, for advice.

B makes a judgment as to the competitive value of the information A is requesting. If it seems to him vital to his own firm's competitive position, he will not provide it. However, if it seems useful but not crucial - and if A seems to be a potentially useful and appropriately knowledgeable expert who may be of future value to B - B will answer his request as well as he can and/or refer him to other experts of his acquaintance. B may go to considerable lengths to help A: He may, for example, run a special simulation for him on his firm's computer system. At the same time, A realizes that in asking for and accepting the help, he is incurring an obligation to provide similar help to B - or to another referred by B - at some future date. No explict accounting of favors given and received is kept, we find, but the obligation to return a favor seems strongly felt by recipients - "... a gift always looks for recompense" (3).

Informal know-how trading can occur between firms which do and do not directly compete. Informal but extensive trading of information with competitive value between direct competitors is perhaps the most interesting case, however, because if we can explain that phenomenon, we can more easily explain trading with less competitive impact. Therefore, we focus much of the ensuing data and discussion on the case of informal know-how trading between direct competitors.

3.0: <u>Case Study: Informal Trading of Proprietary Process</u>
<u>Know-How Among US "Minimill" Steel Producers</u>

To date, our study of informal know-how trading among
competitors is most complete in the instance of process know-how
trading among competing US minimill steel producers. We offer
this data here as an existence test of the general phenomenon we
are discussing, and as a means of conveying its flavor.

Minimills, unlike "integrated" steel plants, do not produce
steel from iron ore. Rather, they begin with steel scrap which
they melt in an electric arc furnace. Then, they adjust the
chemistry of the molten steel, cast it in continuous casters and
roll it into steel shapes. Modern facilities and relatively low
labor, capital and materials costs have enabled US steel minimill
firms to compete extremely effectively against the major integrated US steel producers in recent years. Indeed, they have
essentially driven US integrated producers out of the market for
many commodity products.

The term minimill is not precisely defined, and is becoming
less so as "minimill" plants grow in size and complexity. Early
minimills were relatively small (50,000 - 150,000 tons per year
capacity) and produced primarily commodity products such as rein-
forcing bar used in the construction industry. Today, however,
some individual plants approach 1,000,000 tons' annual capacity
and many are reaching far beyond commodity products into forging
quality, alloy steel, stainless steel and "nearly any steel
grade capable of being melted in an electric furnace" (4).

There are approximately 60 steel minimill plants (and
approximately 40 producers) in the US today. The most produc-
tive of these have surpassed their Japanese competitors in terms
of tons of steel per labor hour input, and are regarded as among
the world leaders in this process.

3.1 <u>Methods</u>

The sample of minimills we studied is a subset of a recent
listing of minimill plants published in <u>Iron and Steel Engineer</u>.

This listing (5) contained 45 US firms with one or more minimill plants. We selected the four firms with the largest annual molten steel production capacity ("melt capacity") from this list, and then added six others selected at random from the same list. Later, some interviewees in these firms suggested that we also study Quanex Corporation (because it was viewed as an industry outlier in terms of trading behavior) and so we also added this firm. All firms included in the study sample are identified in Table 1.

Table 1: US Steel Minimill Firm Sample

STEEL MINIMILL FIRM	MELT CAPACITY[a] (Tons/Year,000)
Four Largest Firms	
Chaparral, Midllothian, TX	1,400
Florida Steel, Tampa, Fla	1,578
North Star, Salt Lake City, UT	2,300
Nucor, Charlotte, NC	2,000
Other (Randomly Selected)	
Bayou Steel, LaPlace, LA	650
Cascade Steel Rolling Mills, McMinnville, OR	250
Charter Electric Melting, Chicago, IL	130
Kentucky Electric Steel, Ashland, KY	280
Marathon Steel, Tempe, Ariz[b]	185
Raritan River Steel, Perth Amboy, NJ	500
Specially Selected Outlier	
Quanex, Houston, TX	

[a] Source: Edward L. Nemeth, "Mini-Midi Mills - U.S., Canada and Mexico", Iron and Steel Engineer 61:6 (June 1984), Table 1, pp. 30-34. [b] Firm closed in July 1985, and is in liquidation.

Interviews were conducted with plant managers and other managers with direct knowledge of manufacturing and manufacturing process engineering at each firm in our study sample. Our questioning, mostly by telephone, was focused by an interview guide, and addressed two areas primarily: (1) Has your firm / does your firm develop proprietary know-how which would be of interest to competitors? If so, give concrete examples of process or product

improvements which you have developed, and some estimate of their value. (2) Do you trade proprietary know-how with competitors? With whom? Do you hold anything back? What? Why? Give concrete examples.

The source of major, well-known innovations claimed by interviewees was cross-checked by asking interviewees in several firms, "Which firm developed x?" The accuracy of self-reported trading behavior could not be so checked. We nevertheless have confidence in the pattern found because interviewees in all but one of the sampled firms provided independent, detailed discussions of very similar trading behavior.

3.2: Results

Personnel at all firms except Quanex (selected for study specifically because its behavior differed from the norm) reported routinely trading proprietary process know-how - sometimes with direct competitors. This finding strikes us as impressive. Conventional wisdom might suggest that know-how trading between competitors is rare. But even if we assume as a null hypothesis that 50% of all minimills will engage in know-how trading, $p < .01$ that trading would be as frequent as we have found it to be in fact.

Table 2: Know-How Trading Patterns

Steel Minimill Firm	In-House Process Devel?	Know-How Trade?
Four Largest Firms		
Chaparral	MAJOR	Yes
Florida Steel	Minor	Yes
North Star	Minor	Yes
Nucor	MAJOR	Yes
Other		
Bayou Steel	Minor	Yes
Cascade Steel	Minor	Yes
Charter Elec	Minor	Yes
Kentucky Electric	Minor	Yes
Marathon Steel	Minor	Yes
Raritan River	Minor	Yes
Quanex	Minor	NO

Interestingly, reported know-how trading often appeared to ✗
go far beyond an arms-length exchange of data at conferences.
Interviewees reported that, sometimes, workers of competing firms
were trained (at no charge), firm personnel were sent to competing facilities to help set up unfamiliar equipment, etc. ⌐

Of course, the firms which report informal know-how trading
with competitors in Table 2 do not trade with every competitor,
and do not necessarily trade with each other. (The interviewed
firms differ widely in technical accomplishment and, as we will
see later, a firm will only offer to trade valuable know-how with
those who can reciprocate in kind.)

Before turning to consider why the trading of proprietary
process know-how occurs in the steel minimill industry, let us
examine that behavior in more detail under three headings:
(1) Did minimills studied in fact develop/have proprietary
process know-how of potential value to competitors; (2) did firms
possessing know-how trade with direct competitors; and (3) was
know-how in fact "traded", as opposed to simply revealed without
expectation of a return of similarly valuable know-how?

3.2.1: Valuable Know-How?

Since many minimill products are commodities, it is logical
that process innovations which save production costs will be of
significant value to innovating firms, and of significant
interest to competitors. Donald Barnett and Louis Schorsch (6)
report US minimill 1981 costs to manufacture wire rod (a reasonably representative commodity minimill product) to be as shown in
Table 3.

On the basis of Table 3 data, it seems reasonable that all
minimills would have a keen interest in know-how which would
reduce their labor and/or energy costs. And, indeed, all
interviewed reported making in-house improvements to methods or
equipment in order to reduce these costs. In addition, some
reported making process innovations which increased the range of
products which they could produce.

Table 3: Minimill Costs Per Ton (Wire Rod, 1981)

Cost Category	Dollars per Ton	Percent of Total
Labor	$60	21%
Steel Scrap	93	33%
Energy	45	16%
Other Operating[a]	65	23%
Total Operating	$263	
Depreciation	11	4%
Interest	7	2%
Misc. Tax	3	1%
TOTAL COSTS[b]	$284	100%

Source: Donald F. Barnett and Louis Schorsch, Steel: Upheaval in a Basic Industry (Cambridge, MA: Ballinger, 1983), Table 4-3, p.95.

[a] Includes alloying agents, refractories, rolls, etc.
[b] Excluding any return on equity.

Nucor and Chaparral conduct major and continuing in-house process development efforts (conducted, interestingly, by their production groups rather than by separate R&D departments). Thus, Nucor is now investing millions in a process to continuously cast thin slabs of steel. If successful, this process will allow minimills to produce wide shapes as well as narrow ones, and will perhaps double the size of the market open to minimill producers - an advance of tremendous value to the industry.

The in-house know-how development efforts of other interviewed minimills is much less ambitious, consisting mainly of relatively small refinements in process equipment and technique. For example, one firm is experimenting with a water-cooled furnace roof which is more horizontal (has less pitch) than that of competitors. (The effect of the flatter furnace roof is expected to be increased clearance and faster furnace loading times, a cost advantage.) Other firms develop modified rollers for their rolling mills which allow them to make better or different steel shapes, and so forth. While many such process refinements have only a small individual impact on production costs, their collective impact can be large (7). (Example: A US

minimill claims a 98% "yield" [good quality output] of steel tubing using the same equipment used by a competing French firm - which can only obtain a 75% yield.)

In sum, then, most steel minimill firms do appear to develop proprietary know-how which would be of significant value to at least some competitors.

3.2.2: Direct Competitors?

Our next question is: Are steel minimill firms which trade know-how really direct competitors? If they are not, of course, the know-how trading behavior we observe becomes more easily explicable: Noncompetitors cannot turn traded proprietary know-how to one's direct disadvantage.[1]

Many minimills do compete with each other today, although this was not always the case. When minimills began to emerge in the late 1950's to late 1960's, they were usually located in smaller regional markets and were protected by transportation costs from severe competition with other minimills. Today, however, there are many minimill firms and significant competition between neighboring plants. In addition, the production capacity of minimill plants has steadily increased, and the larger facilities "define their markets as widely as do integrated [steel mill] facilities" (8).

Some minimill interviewees report that they do trade know-how with personnel from directly competing plants. Others report that they "try to" avoid direct transfer to competitors - but are aware that they cannot control indirect transfer. (Since traders cannot control the behavior of those who acquire their information, the noncompeting firms they select to trade with may later transfer that information to competitors.)

---

[1] Firms which produce identical products may not be direct competitors for many reasons. For example, firms may be restricted to a regional market by the economics of transport (e.g., liquified industrial gases, fresh milk products) or by regulation (e.g., banks).

3.2.3: Is It Really Trading?

Proprietary know-how is only a subject for trading if free diffusion can be prevented. Therefore we asked interviewees: "Could the proprietary know-how you develop in-house be kept secret if you wanted to do this?"

In the instance of know-how embodied in equipment visible in a plant tour, free diffusion was considered hard to prevent. Many people visit minimill plants. Members of steelmaking associations visit by invitation, and association members include competitors. In principle, such visits could be prevented, but the value of doing so is unclear, since two other categories of visitors could not be as easily excluded. First, suppliers of process equipment often visit plants for reasons ranging from sales to repair to advice. They are expert at detecting equipment modification, and are quick to diffuse information around the industry. Second, customers often request plant tours in order to assure themselves of product quality, and may notice and/or request information on process changes.

On the other hand, interviewees seem to believe that they can effectively restrict access to know-how if they really want to, and there is evidence for this on a general level. Thus, Nucor and Chaparral both attempt to exert some control over their process innovations, and interviewees at other firms think they have some success. Quanex does not allow plant visits at all, and feels it effectively protects its know-how thereby.

Data on this matter is also available at the level of specific innovations, although we have not yet collected it systematically. As an example, however, a firm with a policy of being generally open reported that it nevertheless was able to successfully restrict access to a minor rolling innovation for several years. (That firm reported gaining an "extra" $140 per ton because it was the only minimill able to roll a particular shape desired by some customers. It apparently only lost control of its innovation when production people explained it to a

competitor at a Bar Mill Association meeting.)

Interviewees, including top management, were aware of know-how exchange patterns in their industry and emphasized that they were not giving know-how away - they were consciously trading information whose value they recognized. Thus, Bayou Steel: "How much is exchanged depends on what the other guy knows - must be reciprocal". Chaparral Steel: "If they don't let us in [to their plant] we won't let them in [to ours] - must be reciprocal". These statements are convincing to us because most interviewees who did engage in information exchange had clearly thought about whom to trade with and why. When asked, they were able to go into considerable detail about the types of firms they did and did not deal with, and why dealing with a given firm would or would not involve a valuable two-way exchange of know-how.

Know-how trading in the steel minimill industry was not centrally controlled beyond the provision of general guidelines by top management. Also, no one was explicitly counting up the precise value of what was given or received by a firm, and a simultaneous exchange of valuable information was not insisted upon. However, in an informal way, participants appeared to strive to keep a balance in value given and received, without resorting to explicit calculation. On average over many transactions, a reasonable balance was probably achieved, although individual errors in judgment are easy to cite. (For example, in the instance of the minor rolling innovation mentioned above, the innovating firm's sales department was furious when, in their view, engineering "simply gave" the unique process know-how, and the associated monopoly profit, away.)

3.2.4: Quanex, The Exception

Quanex was the sole exception to the minimill trading norm which we found. The firm was not on the list of minimills which we used to generate our sample, and we only became aware of it and its outlier status because we routinely asked each firm

interviewed if it knew of any firm whose trading behavior
differed from its own. Quite possibly, Quanex is the only
industry outlier with respect to know-how trading behavior.
Certainly, it is the only one our interviewees knew of.

When contacted, Quanex explained its behavior by saying
that, first, it did not trade because it felt it had nothing to
learn from competing firms (a contention disputed by some
interviewees). Second, it said that, while it did produce steel
by a minimill-like process, it produced specialty steels and
considered its competitors to be other specialty steel producers
(e.g., Timkin) and not minimills. And, Quanex reported, it was
not an outlier with respect to specialty steel producers where,
it said, secrecy rather than trading was the norm. (We think
this latter point very interesting, but will not pursue it
here. If confirmed, it suggests that know-how trading patterns
may differ between closely related industries. This in turn
opens the way to empirical study of the underlying causes of
know-how trading under well-controlled conditions.)

3.3: Other Empirical Evidence Regarding Know-How Trading

Is know-how trading unique to the US minimill industry? Or
is it a significant form of R&D cooperation in many industries?
At the moment, I am aware of only three sources of empirical data
on this important matter - and all tend to suggest that informal
know-how trading exists in many industries.

First, my students and I have now conducted pilot interviews
in several US industries in addition to steel minimills. And, on
an anecdotal basis, I can report that we have found informal
know-how trading apparently quite common in some industries,
and essentially absent in others. Thus, self-report by interviewees suggests that trading is widespread among aerospace
firms and waferboard manufacturing mills, but rare or absent
among powdered metals fabricators and producers of the biological
enzyme klenow. (Interestingly, however, trading seems a more
quasi-covert, secretive activity by engineering staffs in some of

these industries than was the case in steel minimills. In minimills, top management was typically aware of trading and approved. This does not seem to be necessarily the case in all industries where significant trading is present.)

Second, data in a study by Thomas Allen, et al. (9), of a sample of Irish, Spanish and Mexican firms appears consistent with what I am calling informal know-how trading. Allen examined the "most significant change, in either product or process" which had occurred in each of 102 firms during recent years. Interviews were conducted with innovation participants to determine the source of the initial idea for the innovation and important sources of help used in implemention. Coding of the data showed that approximately 23% of the important information in these categories came from some form of personal contact with "apparent competitors" (firms in the same industry).

T. Allen elaborates on the behavior observed:

> In a typical scenario, the manager from one of these firms might visit a trade show in another country, and be invited on plant visit by representatives of a [competing] foreign firm. While there he would encounter some new manufacturing technique that he would later introduce into his own firm. In other cases managers approached apparently competing firms in other countries directly and were provided with surprisingly free access to their technology (10).

Third, Robert Allen (11) reports "collective invention" in the nineteenth-century English steel industry, and we think that this might in fact be an example of informal know-how trading. Allen begins by exploring progressive change in two important attributes of iron furnaces during 1850-1875 in England's Cleveland district: an increase in the height of furnace chimneys, and an increase in the temperature of the "blast" air pumped into an iron furnace during operation. Both types of technical change resulted in a significant and progressive improvement in the energy efficiency of iron production. Next, he examines technical writings of the time, and finds that at least some who built new furnaces reaching new chimney heights

and/or blast temperatures publicly revealed data on their furnace
design and performance in meetings of professional societies and
in published material. That is, some firms revealed data of
apparent competitive value to both existing and potential
competitors.

The essential difference between know-how trading and what
Allen calls collective invention is that know-how trading
involves an exchange of valuable information between competitors,
while collective invention requires that all competitors and
potential competitors be given free access to proprietary
know-how (14). Allen finds that this free access requirement
presents interpretive difficulties, however.[2]

As will be seen later when we discuss the causes of know-how
trading, the difficulty Allen notes is not present if the iron
manufacturers he examined were actually engaged in know-how
trading rather than in collective invention. This seems to us
possible. Allen deduced that technical data was made available
to all because he observed that much was published and presented
to technical societies. Certainly, what was published was
public: But know-how with trading value might well have been
withheld from publication and/or published only when it -

---

[2] The interpretive difficulty reported by Allen:

It is extremely puzzling why firms released
design and cost information to potential entrants to
the industry. If (as we continue to assume) the
industry was competitively organized, it would appear
that this action could only rebound to the disadvantage
of the firm. To the degree that the information
release accelerated technical progress, the price of
the product would decline and so would the net income
of the firm that released the information (15).

Allen proposes three possible explanations for such behavior
(a firm's desire to publicize its accomplishment even at the
penalty of lost profit; a firm's inability to keep the know-how
secret even if it wished to; speculations regarding special
conditions under which a firm might possibly find the open
revealing of know-how to be profitable), but the puzzle is not
convincingly laid to rest.

eventually - lost proprietary status. Both of these suggested behaviors would be difficult to discern via written records but are, in fact, part of the trading behavior of present-day firms.

4.0: An Economic Explanation for Know-How Trading

We propose that it may be possible to explain both the presence and absence of informal trading of proprietary know-how between direct competitors in terms of private economic benefit accruing to competing firms. We begin by framing the phenomenon in the context of a Prisoner's Dilemma, and then initially explore the plausibility of such a model by reference to the small amount of real-world information currently available to us.

4.1: Know-How Trading as a Prisoner's Dilemma

Firms which trade proprietary know-how appear to make each trading decision on a situation-specific basis, that is, "Shall I trade this with that firm?" Therefore, the case of know-how trading between competitors may be considered as an example of a two-party "Prisoner's Dilemma". The essence of such situations is that the two parties involved in the Dilemma are likely to achieve the highest private gain over many interactions, "moves in the game", if they cooperate. Each player is continuously tempted to "defect" from cooperation, because he will reap higher returns from a single move if he defects while his partner behaves cooperatively. But if he yields to this temptation for short-run gain and defects, his partner may well respond by defections of his own in succeeding moves. Axelrod (12) has shown that strategies involving defections as opposed to cooperation tend to lower the long-term returns of both players.

Two conditions must hold for a situation to be defined as a Prisoner's Dilemma. The first is that the value of the four possible outcomes must be T > R > P > S, where: T is the payoff to the player who defects while the other cooperates; R is the payoff to both players when both cooperate; P is the payoff to

both players when both defect; and, finally, S is the payoff to
the player who cooperates when the second player defects. The
second condition is that an even chance for each player to
exploit and be exploited on successive turns of the game does not
result in as profitable an outcome to players as does continuing
mutual cooperation (e.g., 2R > T + S).

Let us begin placing know-how trading in the context of a
Prisoner's Dilemma by specifying that the net benefit (B) of
a proprietary "unit" of know-how to a firm (player) developing
that know-how is:

(1) $$B = NP + MP - C$$

In this equation, NP is the normal profit which a firm may
expect from implementing a "unit" of know-how when its trading
partner has it too. MP is the extra increment of profit (monopoly profit) which a firm can expect to garner if it does not
trade the unit of proprietary know-how, but rather possesses it
exclusively. Finally, C is the cost to an innovating (or
imitating) firm to develop the unit of know-how absent trading.

4.1.1: A Base Case

As a base case, assume that in each play of the game, two
firms each start out with one unit of proprietary know-how unique
to it. Assume also that each of these two units, although
different, has identical NP, MP and C associated with it.
Then, each firm starts with proprietary know-how having a
pre-play value of NP + MP - C. Because knowledge is the good
being traded here, a cooperative trade, R, between the two firms
will result in each firm having both units of know-how post-
trade, and each having the following post-trade benefit :

(2) $$B = 2NP - C$$

That is, post-trade each will have lost its monopoly profit with

respect to the other which was associated with exclusive possession of its own know-how unit, but will have gained the benefit
of an additional know-how unit without associated development
cost. Similar reasoning allows us to work out the consequences
of all four possible outcomes of a single play of the game by the
two firms as:

(3) $T=2NP+MP-C$, $R=2NP-C$, $P=NP+MP-C$, and $S=NP-C$.

According to the terms of the Prisoner's Dilemma, cooperation is the most profitable long-term strategy of each of the
two firms considering its options if the two conditions described
earlier are met. We see from (1), above, that both condition 1
($T > R > P > S$) and condition 2 ($2R > T+S$) hold if $NP > MP$.
Therefore, if $NP > MP$ a policy of know-how trading will usually
pay better in the long run than any other strategy. On the other
hand, both conditions fail and continuing defection or no
exchange is the best option if $NP < MP$.

The simple model just given can obviously be brought into
more precise alignment with the real world if we add refinements. For example, Mansfield (13) has found that the cost of
imitation is typically lower than the cost of an original
innovation. Also, a firm does not typically lose all monopoly
benefit from an innovation by revealing it to (trading it with)
just one competitor if that competitor keeps it secret in turn.
Instead, MP probably progressively declines as the innovation
is progressively spread to more competitors.

But, since at this point we have only anecdotal data to use
in testing the model, it is reasonable to defer complexity.
Instead, we will attempt to assess the intuitive plausibility of
the simple model by reference to real-world examples.

4.1.2: When Proprietary Know-How Offers
Little Competitive Advantage

In essence, NP > MP holds when the exclusive possession of
a know-how "unit" offers relatively little competitive advantage. This is often the case in the real world, we suggest. To
understand why, it is important to first understand a little more
about the actual nature of most (not all) proprietary know-how.

"Know-how" may have the ring of something precious and
nonreproducible to the nontechnical reader. In fact, however,
most proprietary know-how shares two characteristics: (1) It is
not vital to a firm, and (2) it can be independently developed by
any competent firm needing it, given an appropriate expenditure
of time and money (14). Consider two examples of such "typical"
proprietary know-how:

> An engineer at an aerospace firm was having trouble
> manufacturing a part from a novel composite material with
> needed precision. He called a professional colleague he
> knew at a competitor and asked for advice. As it happens,
> the competitor had solved the problem by experimenting and
> developing some process know-how involving mold design and
> processing temperatures, and he willingly passed along this
> information.

It was certainly convenient for the firm now facing the
difficulty to learn of a solution from the competitor - but
it was not in any way vital. First, it was possible to struggle
along without solving the problem at all. The part was in fact
being made, but with a high scrap rate and much effort. Second,
the engineer assigned to solve this problem was competent and
could certainly develop a solution independently given appropriate time and funds.

> Process engineers at a manufacturer of waferboard (a
> fabricated wood product somewhat like plywood) were having
> trouble involving frequent "jamming" of a production machine
> with wood being processed. As it happens, competitors had
> solved this problem by experimenting and developing some
> process know-how involving the regulation of wood moisture
> content. When contacted, they passed along what they had
> learned.

Again, it was convenient for the firm now facing the difficulty to know this solution, but it was not essential or even very important. First, the cost of struggling on without solving the problem at all was not exorbitant: Machine operators could continue to cope simply by stopping the troublesome machine and clearing it as often as necessary. Second, a competent engineer assigned to solve this problem could certainly solve it independently.

When proprietary know-how does have the attributes just described, one can perhaps intuitively see the plausibility of our model's prediction that competing firms will find it profitable to engage in know-how trading. Conceptually, the consequences of noncooperation in know-how sharing under such conditions are similar to those of a policy of not cooperating in sharing spare parts with direct competitors who use an identical process machine. An industrywide policy of noncooperation among competitors with respect to spares would under most circumstances not permanently deprive any firm of needed spares, nor otherwise significantly affect the competitive position of firms in the industry. It would simply result in increased downtime and/or spares-stocking costs for all - a net loss for all relative to the consequences of a policy of cooperation.

4.1.3: When Proprietary Know-How Offers Significant Competitive Advantage

Sometimes, the competitive value of a unit of know-how is large, and MP > NP. According to our model, we would then expect that informal know-how trading would not occur. We can illustrate this possibility with two especially interesting examples, which appear to show know-how trading behavior shifting as the value of a given type of know-how shifts over time.

First, aerospace engineer interviewees have informed us that they freely exchange most know-how under "normal" conditions. But, when a competition for an important government contract is

in the offing the situation changes, and trading of information between competitors which might affect who wins the contract stops. Later, after the contract has been awarded, the same know-how which was recently closely guarded will apparently again be traded freely.

The reported behavior seems reasonable. Much aerospace know-how has the characteristics discussed in the previous section: It is not critical, and, under "normal conditions" it can be independently reproduced by competent engineers if need be. Therefore, it is likely that NP > MP, for such know-how, and that know-how trading would therefore pay according to our model. But, when a competition for an important government contract is near, conditions are not normal. Often, there will not be enough time to produce needed know-how independently, and therefore the MP value of a given piece of competition-related know-how could increase temporarily. If the increase reached the point where NP < MP, it is reasonable according to our model that know-how trading temporarily stop – the behavior in fact reported by interviewees. And, of course, after the contract is awarded it is reasonable that the MP value of competition-related know-how will drop and trading resume, as interviewees report that it does.

Second, we are told that geologists working for competing oil companies often informally trade geological data under "normal conditions". However, when acreage will be subject to competitive bidding for oil leases within a few weeks, trading of data on that acreage stops. Again, this behavior seems reasonable in terms of our model.

Here, the logic behind the observed shift in trading behavior appears to us to be identical to that presented in instance of the aerospace example just discussed. In this case, some "proprietary" geological data collected by major oil companies is usually not of major competitive value (NP > MP), because any firm which knows it wants a particular data set can hire a contractor to collect it within a few weeks. However, if

acreage will be subject to competitive bidding within a few weeks, a competitor would not have time to generate needed data afresh, and the firm with exclusive possession of critical data may have a significant competitive advantage (NP < MP). Again, therefore, the reported shift in know-how trading behavior makes sense in terms of our simple model.

In both of the examples just given, the know-how at issue could have been independently redeveloped by anyone who wanted it. But the know-how nonetheless yielded competitive advantage to its possessor because the time needed for independent redevelopment was simply not available. Sometimes, however, know-how which can yield a major competitive advantage cannot be routinely reinvented. Then NP < MP for years, and trading of that know-how may never be in the best interests of the firm possessing it.

4.1.4: When Proprietary Know-How Offers No Competitive Advantage

There are many real-world conditions where unique possession of proprietary know-how offers essentially no competitive advantage to a firm relative to firms producing the same good or service. (For example, electrical and gas utilities produce the same product but serve different geographic areas and so do not compete.) We would expect know-how trading to be to the advantage of firms in such a situation, and therefore would predict it to occur. Anecdotal evidence available to this point supports this prediction, but is certainly only of illustrative value. (For example, on the basis of interviews we find that electric and gas utilities do appear to share know-how extensively.)

4.1.5: When Proprietary Know-How Has Negative Competitive Value

In at least some real-world conditions, it appears that competition is enhanced by an exchange in know-how. As an example, consider that the establishment of uniform standards in a product category can sometimes enlarge markets and benefit all participating manufacturers. (Recent examples include standards set for computer networks and compact audio disks.) The estab-

lishment of standards requires some sharing of know-how by participating firms. As a second example consider the sharing of proprietary information on safety hazards between competitors, such as the recent sharing of information on Dioxin among competitors in the chemical industry.

4.1.6: If Traders Have Different Amounts of Know-How

Our pilot research investigations to date show several instances in which the large, relatively innovative firms in a product category examined appear to energetically suppress trading by their employees, while smaller producers of the same product types appear less restrictive. Examples are Kraft in cheese products, IBM in computers, P&G in paper goods. On the other hand, this pattern does not appear in our study of steel minimill firms, where the better-endowed firms seemed to simply pick trading partners who were equally well-endowed. Both patterns can be explained by the operation of either or both of the two following factors:

(1) The firms which are better-endowed feel that they have all the know-how they need in-house. Therefore they would not receive any benefit from trading with competitors and do not do so.

(2) A firm which has more proprietary know-how than potential trading partners will, assuming know-how of equal absolute value is exchanged in a trade, be worse off in percentage-of-unique-know-how-held terms relative to competitors than it was pre-trading. This could reasonably cause a relative reluctance by better-endowed firms to trade with those having less proprietary know-how. Consider a pre-trade situation in which firm A has $n+1$ know-how packets and all other firms have n packets. Assume that all firms make M trades.

	Know-How Ratio	Pre-Trade		Post-Trade
(4)	$\dfrac{\text{Firm A}}{\text{competitors}}$	$\dfrac{n+1}{n}$	$>$	$\dfrac{n+1+M}{n+M}$

From (4), we also see that the larger the pre-trade discrepancy in the amount of proprietary know-how possessed by two firms considering a trade, the worse the ratio of relative gains from exchange becomes for the better-endowed firm (assuming know-how units of equal absolute value are exchanged).

4.1.7: Trading Strategies

Know-how trading deals with the trading of knowledge. As a consequence, some trading strategies are possible which are not envisioned in the usual Prisoner's Dilemma. A firm receiving know-how in trade does not care who originally developed it; he only cares that it has value to him. One important criterion of value is that the know-how must be novel to the recipient - there is no value in getting the same information twice. As a consequence, firms can in principle adopt trading strategies which yield a greater benefit than simple, long-term cooperation. For example, a firm might find that a strategy of rapid trading pays. Such a strategy might allow the firm to exchange its know-how and the know-how developed by others which it obtained from earlier trades to firms which still find that know-how novel, a trading advantage. Whether or not such strategies are used under real-world conditions we do not yet know.

Firms may also adopt strategies of restricting know-how trading to only a subset of all the firms in their industry for some competitive purpose. For example, US or Japanese semiconductor producers may decide it is to their advantage to trade know-how with other domestic firms but not with foreign firms - or vice versa. Strategies of this kind certainly are practiced in the real world.

5.0: Informal Know-How Trading In Context

Informal technology trading can usefully be compared with
and contrasted to two other forms of R&D exchange between firms:
(1) agreements to perform R&D cooperatively; (2) agreements to
license or sell proprietary technical knowledge. As we will see,
informal know-how trading can usefully be seen as an inexpensive,
flexible form of cross-licensing. Under appropriate conditions,
it appears to function better than either of these better-known
alternatives.

Agreements to trade or license know-how involve firms in
less uncertainty than do agreements to perform R&D cooperatively. This is because the former deals with existing knowledge of
known value which can be exchanged quickly and certainly. In
contrast, agreements to perform R&D offer future know-how
conditioned by important uncertainties as to its value and the
likelihood that it will be delivered at all. (The value of the
know-how contracted for is uncertain because R&D outcomes
cannot be predicted with certainty. The delivery of the results
of cooperative R&D projects to sponsoring firms is somewhat
uncertain because such results are best transferred back to the
sponsoring firms in the minds of employees participating in the
cooperative research. Given the US tradition of frequent job
changes, participants run significant risk of losing the benefits
of their investment by losing the employee[s] they assigned to
the project.)

Informal know-how trading such as we have observed empirically has a lower transaction cost than more formal agreements to
license or sell similar information. Transaction costs in
informal know-how trading systems are low because decisions to
trade or not trade proprietary know-how are made by individual,
knowledgeable engineers. No elaborate evaluations of relative
benefit or seeking of approvals from firm bureaucracies are
involved. Although informal, each engineer's assessment of
the relative likely value of the trades he elects to make may be

quite accurate: An information seeker can tell on the basis of his first interaction whether the expert advice he is given is of good quality - because he will immediately seek to apply it. An information provider can test the level of the inquirer's expertise and future value as a source of information by the nature and subtlety of the questions asked. Also, although a particular informal judgment of the value of a trade may be quite incorrect, many small transactions are typically made. Therefore, the net value of proprietary process know-how given and received will probably not be strongly biased for or against any participating firm.

In general, we may say that informal know-how exchange between competing and noncompeting firms is the most effective form of cooperative R&D when (1) the needed know-how exists in the hands of some member of the trading network, and when (2) the know-how is proprietary only by virtue of its secrecy, and when (3) the value of a particular traded module is too small to justify an explicit negotiated agreement to sell, license or exchange. (Taken together, conditions 2 and 3 have the effect of insuring that the know-how recipient will be free to use the information he obtains without fear of legal intervention by the "donor" firm.) Since much technical knowledge key to progress consists of small, incremental advances, the universe bounded by these three conditions is likely to be a substantial one.

Formal know-how sale or licensing is likely to be preferred when the know-how in question (1) already exists and (2) is of considerable value relative to the costs of a formal transaction. (Experts in the oil and chemical industry report that they engage in formal licensing and sale rather than informal exchange precisely because the value of the know-how in question is typically very high.)

Agreements to perform cooperative R&D must be the form of cooperation of choice when (1) the needed information does not exist within any firm willing to trade, license or sell, and when (2) individual firms do not find it worthwhile to develop

modules of the needed know-how independently. (This would occur when know-how modules have no profitable applications as modules. Perhaps this is often the case, but we are not sure. Perhaps most "new" know-how in fact consists largely of existing modules of know-how developed for other purposes.)

6.0: Summary

Informal know-how trading among direct competitors appears widespread in the real world, and appears to have interesting properties. Further research would seem to offer results of interest to both researchers and practitioners.

Researchers may find that an increased understanding of informal know-how trading opens the way to a more explicit evaluation of the value of competition versus cooperation in the many different areas in which firms must develop proprietary know-how. To the extent that the categories of know-how considered to be of competitive importance can be identified and assessed, it may be possible to develop and explore generic "efficient" competitive strategies which involve both competition and cooperation.

If an increased understanding of efficient competition can allow firms to see some areas of R&D investment as not being of competitive value, or as offering only "redundant" competitive advantage, they might find it profitable to cooperate in more aspects of know-how development. This would lead to a drop in the cost of a given level of competition – a net social gain. Also, if firms understood the benefits of know-how trading better, they might be able to improve current practice of the art. (In many firms, know-how trading is officially frowned upon even though, in our judgment, it may of value to the firm. When this is so, trading may be completely suppressed or carried out in a furtive and inefficient manner.)

29

References

(1) Richard R. Nelson, "The Simple Economics of Basic Scientific Research - A Theoretical Analysis", Journal of Political Economy 67 (June 1959), pp. 297-306.

(2) P. S. Johnson, Co-Operative Research in Industry: An Economic Study (New York, NY: John Wiley & Sons, 1973).

(3) The Havamal, with Selections from other Poems in the Edda, as quoted by Marcel Mauss in The Gift: Forms and Functions of Exchange in Archaic Societies, trans. Ian Cunnison (Glencoe, IL: The Free Press, 1954), p. xiv. Mauss makes a study of patterns of gift giving in a number of cultures, and finds the practice typically associated with strong obligations for recompense to be provided by the recipient of a "gift".

(4) Edward L. Nemeth, "Mini-Midi Mills - U.S., Canada and Mexico", Iron and Steel Engineer 61:6 (June 1984), p. 27.

(5) Ibid., Table 1, pp. 30-34.

(6) Donald F. Barnett and Louis Schorsch, Steel: Upheaval in a Basic Industry (Cambridge, MA: Ballinger, 1983), Table 4-3, p. 95.

(7) Authors who have empirically studied the net impact on productivity of minor process improvements find it to be large. See, especially, Samuel Hollander, The Sources of Increased Efficiency: A Study of Du Pont Rayon Plants (Cambridge, MA: MIT Press, 1965); and K. E. Knight, "A Study of Technological Innovation: The Evolution of Digital Computers", unpublished Ph.D. dissertation, Carnegie Institute of Technology, Pittsburgh, PA, 1963.

(8) Barnett and Schorsch, Steel: Upheaval in a Basic Industry, p. 85.

(9) Thomas J. Allen, Diane B. Hyman, and David L. Pinckney, "Transferring Technology to the Small Manufacturing Firm: A Study of Technology Transfer in Three Countries," Research Policy 12 (1983), pp. 199-211.

(10) Ibid., p. 202.

(11) Robert C. Allen, "Collective Invention", Journal of Economic Behavior and Organization 4 (1983), pp. 1-24.

(12) Robert Axelrod, The Evolution of Cooperation (New York: Basic Books, 1984).

30

(13) Edwin Mansfield, John Rapoport, et al., "Social and Private Rates of Return from Industrial Innovations", _Quarterly Journal of Economics_, 91 (May 1977), pp. 221-40.

(14) See studies on the technical risk associated with R&D project portfolios (References to come).

(15) R. Allen, "Collective Invention," p. 2.

(16) Ibid., p. 16.

www.ingramcontent.com/pod-product-compliance
Lightning Source LLC
LaVergne TN
LVHW011212170225
803859LV00002B/330